Du Good

The Journey Begins

Vincent Schweit

Table of Contents

Chapter 1 - Meet Du   1

Chapter 2 - Call me GO!   12

Chapter 3 - Hey little homie…   24

Chapter 4 - Be our own Biggest Fan!   46

Chapter 5 - Quokka Giraffe?   64

Introduction

'Du Good' is a series of books, that follow the adventures of a Quokka [kwaa-*kuh*] named Du [do]. Du's finding it hard to Love himself, believing what others say about him to be true.

This journey also has activities, and by completing them we can help too. So follow along as the journey begins, the journey of a Quokka named Du.

The activity books are available to download from the following links:

g-level.love/downloads

or

g-level.love (then select the downloads tab)

Chapter 1 - Meet Du

Meet Du, he's a Quokka,
They're the happiest animals on earth.
Du's favorite thing is to smile,
And he's been that way since birth.

His favorite color is blue,
So of course so are his clothes.
And he always has a backpack on,
Preparing for anything, I suppose.

But lately Du feels different,
And his smile is fading away.
Not because he doesn't like to smile,
It's the judgments others say.

He tries to hide it the best he can,
And keeps his smile shining bright.
But no one knows on the inside,
The battles he's trying to fight.

See, Du has always loved himself,
From his shiny black nose, to his big brown eyes.
But lately Du's getting picked on,
Now instead of smiling he just wants to cry.

A couple of kids called him fat last week,
Which hurt his feelings and made him sad.
Now when Du looks in the mirror or eats,
His smile goes away and he feels really bad.

But that's just the beginning though,
Now Du's starting to believe it too.
So his smile has gone away completely,
Because he believes what they said is true!

Then one day Du is walking in the forest,
With his head down, looking like he just cried.
When he hears the kids that called him fat coming,
He starts to panic, and looks for a place to hide.

First he sees a small bush,
But thinks, "Not there, I'm way too big."
Then as he's looking for other places,
He takes a step back and breaks a twig.

Du is scared they might have heard him,
So he quickly jumps behind a tree.
Then listens close as they pass him by,
His eyes closed so tight he cannot see.

With a sigh of relief Du opens his eyes,
And is almost blinded by a glare.
It looks like a half buried treasure chest,
Du wonders, "Why would that be there?"

As he opens the chest he notices,
It contains just a single book.
So Du picks it up and takes it out,
To get a closer look.

There's a black symbol on the gold cover,
It's a letter G with an L attached below.
Then there's a question mark right above the L,
What it means, Du really wants to know.

Du thinks, "I wonder who this belongs to,
And if they'd mind if I take a look?"
But he's so excited to see what's in it,
So Du begins to open the book.

Activity

Meet Du he's a Quokka. They're known as being the happiest animals on earth because of their smiles!

However, Du's smile has been fading away lately. He's beginning to believe the judgments that others say about him are true. Then, Du opens his eyes to see a treasure chest containing a single book!

Let's take this journey with Du and start by showing him how we smile!

Let's help Du find his smile. Write five things that make us smile, and let's smile while writing them!

1.

2.

3.

4.

5.

Coloring Activity

Ever since Du was called fat, he's been feeling sad.

Du is almost blinded by the glare of a treasure chest.

Du finds a treasure chest containing a book with a symbol on it!

Chapter 2 - Call me GO!

The first page shows a bear,
With one hand held right under its chin.
It looks like it's thinking of something,
And its face has on a grin.

Under the bear reads 'Think Good',
But Du doesn't believe that he can.
All he can think of is being called fat,
Then he sees, 'Be our own Biggest Fan'.

It's the only sentence on the next page,
And Du wonders if it's something he can do.
Then Du gets scared and drops the book,
As an owl swoops in and says "Whooo".

"Whoo are you?" the owl asks.
Du replies, "Hello, my name is Du."
"Well I'm Gary Owl, but call me GO," he says,
"It's very nice to meet you!"

"It's nice to meet you too GO", Du replies.
"I just found this treasure chest by the tree.
It only has one book in it though,
So I wanted to open it up and see.

"The first page says to 'Think Good',
Then to 'Be our own Biggest Fan'.
I wish I knew how to do that GO,
But I just don't believe that I can."

"If we set our own limits, we have to keep them," says GO.
"And I don't know about you,
But I don't want to keep my limits.
Do you want to keep your limits Du?"

"I don't want to keep my limits," Du replies
"I just don't know how to change.
Ever since these kids had called me fat,
I've felt different and very strange.

"It's even hard for me to smile now,
And I keep thinking I'm fat in my head.
So I'm not sure how to 'Think Good',
I just keep thinking of what they said."

Go says, "But now you found this book to help you,
With being our own biggest fan.
And remember even if we walk ten miles,
The very first step is where we began.

"I know someone that can help you Du,
He practices baseball at the park.
I fly by and see him every day,
He stays out there until it gets dark.

"His name is Meek and he's a monkey,
I met him when he was on a quest.
You should probably ask him about 'Think Good',
Before you start to read the rest."

Du replies, "Thank you very much GO,
I'll go look for Meek today.
It's going to get dark soon though,
So I should probably be on my way."

Du puts the book in his backpack,
And starts walking towards the park.
He knows he has to hurry to get there,
Because it's close to getting dark.

But as Du's walking he notices something,
And decides to stop and take a look.
It's an elephant wearing an orange beanie,
That has the GL symbol on it from the book.

Activity

Right before Gary Owl (or, as they call him, GO) swoops in, Du opens the book and sees a picture of a bear holding one hand under its chin. Under the bear reads "Think Good" and the next page has one sentence that reads, "Be our own Biggest Fan!"

Du wants to be his own Biggest Fan, but he is setting his own limits! Lucky for Du, GO knows someone that can help!

Currently, Du is setting his own limits, and is not sure how we can "Be our own Biggest Fan" yet. Let's help Du by sharing what we believe it means to "Be our own Biggest Fan"!

1.

Coloring Activity

Du opens the book and sees 'Think Good'.

GO swoops in as Du begins to read the book.

Du is not sure how to "Think Good" yet.

Chapter 3 - Hey little homie…

The elephant has his eyes closed,
And he's taking deep breaths in and out.
Du doesn't want to disturb him,
But he's curious what this is about.

Just then the elephant opens his eyes,
And looks at the forest like a brand new place.
He looks around at every bug, tree, and flower,
With the biggest smile all over his face.

As he looks to the left,
He sees Du standing by a tree.
He smiles even more and says,
"Hey little homie, my name is Ernie."

Ernie's smile is contagious,
So Du can't help but to smile too.
He wants to ask him about the symbol,
But instead says, "Hello, my name is Du.

"What were you doing", Du asks,
"When taking deep breaths in and out?"
Ernie looks at Du and says,
"Clearing my mind of all the doubt.

"It's a practice called meditation,
Used to calm our body and mind.
We just focus on our breathing,
And the present moment is what we find."

"What is the present moment?" Du asks.
Ernie says, "It's giving full attention to this moment now.
To hear, but ignore, all the negative thoughts,
And fill our mind with the thoughts we allow.

"To stop and smell a rose or flower,
And to feel our cheeks every time we smile.
Knowing this very moment is all we have,
And just cherishing it for a while.

"As soon as we focus on the present moment,
The negative thoughts will go away.
Because thinking about the past or future,
Is the only way those thoughts can stay."

"Can you teach me how to meditate?" Du asks,
"So I can be present just like you?
Because the negative thoughts keep saying I'm fat,
And I'm starting to believe that they're true."

Ernie says, "One thing about our thoughts Du,
Is we get to choose the ones that stay.
So choose the thoughts that we Love ourself,
Regardless of how much we weigh.

"Meditation can help to bring us present,
But Loving ourself must come from within.
And knowing the present moment is all we have,
That means *now* is the best time to begin."

Du says, "I'm ready to begin now Ernie,
For the negative thoughts to go away.
To bring myself present and Love myself,
No matter what the thoughts might say."

Ernie says, "We start by sitting comfortably,
And gently closing our eyes.
Then focus on only our breathing,
As the noise in the background dies."

"I'm not sure what to do Ernie", Du says,
"Negative thoughts are flooding my mind."
Ernie replies, "Just sit back and observe them,
Like there's a wall of glass that you're behind.

"No need to fight or judge our thoughts,
Just let them come and go.
And when we realize our mind is wandering,
Focus on taking a deep breath, nice and slow.

"Feel our breath enter our body,
And our stomach move up and down.
Then pay attention to each of our breaths,
Then start with ten and begin to count down."

Du says, "I'm paying attention to each breath,
But the thoughts keep coming back."
Ernie smiles saying,"Focus on the next breath,
And that will put you back on track.

"The secret is always in our breathing,
To be present in this moment right now.
The more we practice the better we get,
Then we can choose the thoughts we allow.

"We don't have to be perfect,
Or get it right the very first try.
Just think of it like a baby bird,
When they first learn how to fly.

"As soon as we've counted down to one,
We can gently open our eyes.
Then pay attention to everything around us,
The dirt, the trees, and the skies."

Du opens his eyes with a smile,
Taking a couple of minutes just looking around.
Everything seems so bright and vibrant,
Then he realizes the sun is going down.

Du says, "I never knew about the present moment,
Now the trees and the skies, they feel brand new.
It's like I'm seeing them for the very first time,
Thank you so much Ernie, I appreciate you!"

Ernie replies, "This is the present moment Du,
Found in every season, every moon, and every hour.
So when we need a reminder to Love ourself,
We can look at the trees, the water, or a flower!"

Du says goodbye to Ernie and knows,
He'll have to go find Meek another day.
Then as he's walking home he starts to think,
"What would my own biggest fan even say?"

Not too long after Du starts thinking,
The negative thoughts start filling his head.
At first he gets sad just listening to them,
Then he remembers what Ernie just said.

So Du starts imagining a wall of glass,
With the negative thoughts trapped on the other side.
Then Du notices a duplicate of himself,
That's curled up in the corner, like he's trying to hide.

Du walks over to help pick himself up, and says,
"We can do this, just believe that we can!"
And for the first time, the negative thoughts disappear,
And Du is finally his own biggest fan!

Du thinks about the wall of glass all night,
Even as he's sitting in the park the next day.
Then as Du is eating his lunch he thinks,
"When I find Meek what should I even say?"

The negative thoughts start taking over again,
Telling Du that Meek will make fun of him too.
He thinks, "As soon as Meek sees me he'll think I'm fat,
And then he'll also believe that it's true!"

Du feels sad, so his eyes start to water,
And he is thinking about running away.
Then out of nowhere a baseball almost hits him,
Then Du hears someone yelling, "Hey!"

Du gets scared and drops his lunch,
Then begins wiping away his tears.
His eyes are still kind of blurry,
But he sees a monkey, with big brown ears.

Activity

Du meets an elephant named Ernie and begins learning about how Self-Love comes from within, and how we can be present when we practice meditation!

Let's show Du what we know about Self-Love! Write two things that we Love about ourself!

1.

2.

Let's show Du how we meditate by breathing in and out, focusing on each breath, while counting down from 10.

Coloring Activity

Du meets Ernie and learns that he was meditating.

To stop and smell a rose or flower!

Everything seems so bright and vibrant after Du meditates.

Chapter 4 - Be our own Biggest Fan!

The monkey says,"Hi I'm Meek, have you seen my ball?
I lost it when I fell from the tree.
I think it may have come this way,
But it was hard for me to see."

Du replies, "Hi Meek I'm Du, and yes I saw your ball,
It landed in front of me and rolled over there."
As Du points to a bush to his left he says,
"And it gave me quite the scare."

"I'm sorry Du, it was an accident", says Meek,
"It's hard to climb with these leg braces, they're new.
I was almost at the top of the tree, but I slipped,
And then the ball got away from me and just flew."

Surprised, Du says, "You seem really calm
After falling from the tree.
I know I'd be scared
If that had happened to me."

Meek smiles and replies, "It's not my first time falling,
Trying to get used to these braces covering my calves.
I honestly got a little embarrassed when I fell,
And I couldn't help but to laugh."

Du frowns saying, "Laughing when you're embarrassed,
Wow, I wish that I could do that.
I remember crying for two whole days once,
After these kids called me fat."

Meek says,"Yes, I know that feeling Du,
I've been made fun of in the past.
But when I realized we can pick ourself up,
I made sure those feelings didn't last.

"I try to focus on one thing mostly,
And that's to be our own biggest fan.
To encourage ourself like we would a friend,
Even when things don't go according to plan.

"I learned the more we cheer ourself on,
The closer we get to achieve,
The dreams and goals we are scared to say,
Or even dare to believe."

Shocked Du asks, "Meek, you have dreams and goals,
That you are scared to say?
Does being our own biggest fan help you,
Make all those fears just go away?"

Meek replies,"It hasn't made the fear go away,
It still pops up in my mind.
But I encourage myself as much as I can,
So the fear gets left behind.

"I figure if we're our own biggest fan,
Whether we're alone or everyone's around,
It won't matter anytime we fall or fail,
We'll encourage ourself whenever we're down.

"So if we get made fun of or embarrassed,
We think, 'What would we say to cheer up a friend?'
Then say the same thing in our own head,
Because what we believe is what matters in the end."

Du takes a few seconds to think about it,
Then asks Meek, in a curious way,
"What did you say when you fell from the tree?
And it's ok if you don't want to say."

Meek looks at Du and smiles saying,
"It's okay Du, I don't mind sharing it with you at all.
First I acted like an umpire and said, 'I'm safe'.
Then I graded it, giving me an eight out of ten on the fall!"

Du laughs and says, "That's awesome!
And that would surely cheer me up.
Is there ever a time when negative thoughts take over?"
Meek immediately replies to Du, "Yup!"

"When we fall or fail, those thoughts sound the loudest,
But remember, for them to be true we have to agree.
So being able to pick ourself up and be our own biggest fan,
Gives us the confidence to be the best we can be."

Du says, "So what you're saying to me Meek,
Is we control the thoughts in our mind.
And we can either choose to believe those thoughts,
Or to leave those thoughts behind?"

Meek smiles back nodding at Du and says,
"Yes that's exactly true!
Because no matter what anyone has to say,
You can always choose to Love you!"

Excitedly Du says, "So say nice things to ourself,
And that will help to pick us up.
Like we would to our best friend,
If they were going through something tough."

"Yes, saying nice things always helps", says Meek,
"And something else that might help too,
Is creating a brand new story in our head,
Like something too funny to even be true."

Du smiles saying,"Thank you for sharing Meek,
I've never thought about that before.
I did want to ask you though, if you don't mind,
What are the leg braces for?"

Meek replies, "You're very welcome Du,
And no, I don't mind that you asked.
They're helping me walk flat on my feet,
So I can play baseball and run really fast.

"My goal is to play baseball with 3P,
He's the best pitcher I've ever seen.
When he was ten, I saw him strike a kid out,
And the kid batting was seventeen!

"These braces will help me run faster,
And be the best that I can be.
I just need more practice getting used to them,
Especially when I'm climbing a tree.

"It's one of my dreams and goals,
Which I used to be scared to say.
Now I practice baseball at the park,
And I'm getting better every day!

"I need to go back to practicing,
But I hope to see you soon.
If you ever want to hang out sometime,
I take a break at the tree every day at noon."

Du smiles saying, "Thank you for the invite Meek,
And explaining what it is you do.
How being our own biggest fan has helped you,
And showing me how it can help me too."

Du walks away with a big smile,
As he's thinking of what Meek said.
He smiles the whole walk home,
And even as he's getting ready for bed.

When Du wakes up the next morning,
He goes into the forest looking for GO.
Then he hears the kids that called him fat coming.
He starts panicking thinking, "Oh no!"

Activity

Du meets a monkey named Meek, and learns more about how we can "Be our own Biggest Fan".

Du learns that we control the thoughts in our mind, and that we can always choose to Love ourself! Meek shares his goal of playing baseball with 3P, and shows Du how we can encourage ourself like we would a friend!

Meek shared one of his goals that he used to be scared to say. Let's share one of our goals with Meek and Du.

1.

Coloring Activity

Du is startled by almost being hit by a baseball.

Meek shares the stories he thought of when he fell from the tree.

Pick ourself up whenever we're down!

Chapter 5 - Quokka Giraffe?

Du starts looking for a place to hide,
But they see him, so it's too late.
Then Nina Hyena looks at him laughing, saying,
"I bet you're hungry even though you just ate!"

Du's cheeks turn red as he feels embarrassed,
And the negative thoughts start flooding his mind.
Then he sees a flower that reminds him of Ernie,
And pictures a wall of glass that he's behind.

Du stands there with his eyes closed,
And begins taking a deep breath in.
With Nina still making fun of him, Du thinks,
"I won't let these negative thoughts win!"

Nina is the main one that bullies Du,
And the others just join in with laughter.
But what Du does next has them all confused,
And they don't know what to do after.

Du starts laughing harder than them,
Then with a smile he just walks away.
Then Nina and the others just stand there,
Confused, they have no idea what to say.

Du can't help but to continue laughing,
As he walks way out of sight.
With a smile on his face the whole time,
He thinks,"Wow, Ernie and Meek were right!"

Du walks to where he found the book,
And searches the trees, but he doesn't see GO.
So he takes a seat on a tree stump,
Still excited, he takes a deep breath and says, "Whoa!"

"I can't believe I did it", Du thinks,
"And the deep breathing really worked too.
It helped calm me down so I could think,
Of something too funny to even be true."

Du closes his eyes and pictures,
The story he thought of that made him laugh.
He thought, "What if I was tall and skinny?"
Then pictured himself part Quokka part Giraffe!

Du starts laughing even harder now,
Just thinking of how long his shirt would be.
He thinks,"I'd rather be exactly who I am,
And start Loving me for just being me."

He thinks about what Ernie told him,
How Loving ourself must come from within.
And he realizes we should Love ourself,
Whether we're big or Quokka Giraffe thin!

Du is sitting on the stump with a smile,
Thinking, "This is the best day I've ever had."
But he can't stop thinking about the book,
He wants to see what's next really, really bad.

Du takes the book out of his backpack,
And turns the page to see what comes next.
He thinks, "'Think Good' was pretty simple,
I wonder if the next page is more complex?"

On the next page there's another bear,
Or at least Du thinks so by the look of its ears.
But he closes the book and jumps up so quick,
Because he's startled by what he hears!

Du hears the bushes rustling,
Like something big is moving around.
He starts to back away from the bush,
And then he hears a growling sound!

Activity

Du sees the kids that called him fat in the forest! As they begin making fun of Du, he sees a flower that reminds him of what he learned from Ernie and Meek.

Then Du shares the story he thought of that made him laugh and to create a different outcome. What can we think about that's too funny to be true?

Let's create and share one story with Du, that we think is too funny to be true!

1.

Coloring Activity

Nina Hyena and the others are confused.

Du learns that we should Love ourself!

Du hears a growling sound coming from the bushes. Who is it??

Made in United States
Orlando, FL
04 September 2023

36498832R00046